RECKLESS

BY CRAIG LUCAS

★ **Revised Edition**

★

DRAMATISTS
PLAY SERVICE
INC.

RECKLESS
Copyright © 1989, 1998, Craig Lucas
Copyright © 1985, Charles Craig Lucas
Copyright © 1984, Charles Craig Lucas
as an unpublished dramatic composition

All Rights Reserved

The play is dedicated to
Daniel Clarke Slautterback

RECKLESS was produced by Circle Repertory (Tanya Berezin, Artistic Director) in New York City, on September 25, 1988. It was directed by Norman Rene; the set design was by Loy Arcenas; the costume design was by Walker Hicklin; the lighting design was by Debra J. Kletter; the sound design was by Stewart Werner; and the production stage manager was Fred Reinglas. The cast was as follows:

RACHEL	Robin Bartlett
TOM	Michael E. Piontek
LLOYD	John Dossett
POOTY	Welker White
ROY	Kelly Connell
TRISH	Susan Blommaert
DOCTORS ONE THROUGH SIX	Joyce Reehling
TIM TIMKO	Kelly Connell
TALK SHOW HOST	Kelly Connell
TALK SHOW GUEST	Welker White
WOMAN PATIENT	Susan Blommaert
TOM JR	Michael E. Piontek

RECKLESS was originally produced in an earlier version by The Production Company, in New York City, May, 1983. It was directed by Norman Rene; the set design was by James Wolk; the costume design was by Steven L Birnbaum; the lighting design was by Debra J. Kletter; and the production stage manager was Bill McComb. The cast was as follows:

RACHEL	Lori Cardille
TOM	Timothy Wahrer
LLOYD	W.T. Martin
POOTY	Maureen Silliman
ROY	James Bormann
BERNADETTE*	Suzanne Henry
TRISH	Susan Blommaert
DOCTORS ONE THROUGH SIX	Patrizia Norcia
TIM TIMKO	James Dupont
TALK SHOW HOST	James Dupont
TALK SHOW GUEST	Suzanne Henry
MAN WITH POOR POSTURE*	James Bormann
WOMAN PATIENT	Susan Blommaert
TOM JUNIOR	Timothy Wahrer

*Role cut from present version.

CHARACTERS

Rachel
Tom
Lloyd
Pooty
Roy
Trish
First Doctor
Tim Timko
Second Doctor
Third Doctor
Fourth Doctor
Fifth Doctor
First Derelict
Second Derelict
Sixth Doctor
Talk Show Host
Sue
Man in Ski Mask
Woman Patient
Receptionist
Tom Junior
Voices of various announcers and newscasters

RECKLESS can be performed with as few as seven actors. TOM, TOM JUNIOR and the MAN IN SKI MASK are doubled, as are the FIRST through SIXTH DOCTORS.

"A solitude ten thousand fathoms deep
Sustains the bed on which we lie, my dear;
Although I love you, you will have to leap;
Our dream of safety has to disappear."

—W. H. Auden

RECKLESS

ACT ONE

Scene 1

The glow of the television. Rachel at the window in her night-gown; Tom in bed.

RACHEL. I think I'm more excited than they are. I really do. I think we just have kids so we can tell them all about Santa Claus and have an excuse to believe it all ourselves again. I really do. They are so excited. I remember that feeling so clearly. I didn't think I could ever sleep. And I remember pinching myself and pinching myself to stay awake so I could hear the reindeers' footsteps, you know? I wanted to believe it so badly. I think that was the last year I did.... Oh God.... Is it still snowing? Why don't you turn the sound up? *(Tom shakes his head, stares at the screen.)* Oh, it's coming down like crazy. You can hear it, can't you, when it gets deep like this? It just swallows up all the sound and you feel like you've been wrapped up in the hands of a big, sweet, giant, white ... monster. Good monster. He's going to carry us away into a dream. My family always had champagne first thing before we opened our presents — I mean, in the morning, you know. I always loved that. I felt like such an adult having champagne and I remember saying to my mother that the bubbles in the champagne looked like snow if you turned your head upside down. I remember thinking I wanted to live in Alaska because it always snowed and Santa was up there, so it must always be Christmas.... You're my Santa Claus. And our two elves. I'm having one of my euphoria at-tacks. I think I'm going to be terminally happy, you'd better watch out, it's catching. Highly contagious.... What's the mat-ter? Just sleepy? *(He nods.)* Can we listen for a second, I won't stay up all night, I promise. *(Rachel switches on the TV.)*

ANNOUNCER'S VOICE. — as they raise their small voices in joyous celebration once more. *(A choir like The Vienna Boys Choir is heard singing.)*

RACHEL. Oh God, look at those faces. I feel so sorry for Jeanette and Freddie sometimes. These things happen for a reason, I know, but ... I always think if something happened to us I'd want them to raise the boys.

ANNOUNCER'S VOICE. This is David Harbinger from Vienna.

SECOND ANNOUNCER'S VOICE. And in a bizarre note this Christmas Eve: an Albanian woman fled across the border into Yugoslavia where it is said she gave birth to a two-headed child today. Both mother and son are reported to be in stable condition. According to spokesmen, the woman is either unwilling or unable to speak. So far there has been no explanation for her flight. Well whoever's dreaming of a white Christmas doesn't have to dream tonight. Weatherman Sheldon Strafford has the story. *(Tom has begun to cry.)*

RACHEL. Isn't that awful?

THIRD ANNOUNCER'S VOICE. Bill, we thought this low pressure front might never move out, but as you can see it finally has and tiny tots and snowmen should be playing together in the streets by dawn.

RACHEL. What's the matter?... Oh, honey, it's just the news, come on, it's not real. We'll turn it off, see? It's gone. *(She switches off TV.)* Don't be upset on Christmas. Everything's great, I'm here and everything's fine.

TOM. I took a contract out on your life.

RACHEL. What do you mean? Life insurance?

TOM. A contract on your life.

RACHEL. That is the sickest joke, I'm sorry. I don't care what's bothering you, you could just come out with it —

TOM. All right, listen to me —

RACHEL. You get these idiotic ideas of what's funny —

TOM. I want you to listen to me if you've never listened to me in your life —

RACHEL. It's Christmas Eve!

TOM. In five minutes a man's going to break through the bay windows downstairs, I'm sorry this is happening this way, it's a stupid solution and we should have talked it out, but it's done and he'll be here in less than five minutes. I want you to put on your coat and some slippers, you can climb out this window over to Jeanette's. When he's gone I'll call you and we can talk about it.

RACHEL. Tom Fitsimmons, I know you and I think this is really off the mark, I'm sorry. Fun is fun ... I'm going to sleep in the other bedroom.

TOM. Rachel! Listen to me now if you want to live!

RACHEL. You're hurting me.

TOM. I paid this man, he's a professional, I cannot take it back. All right, look: *(He produces a handgun.)* This is a .38. It has no bullets. It's staged to look like he broke in and I pulled a gun and he killed you — a thief — an accident. I'm sorry, you can't be here, we'll talk it all out in a little while when he's gone.

RACHEL. You're frightening me.

TOM. I'll tell him you went to stay with your mother. He has his money, he can go. Tell Jeanette we had a fight, it doesn't matter, I'll call you when he's gone.

RACHEL. This is so mean. *(The sound of glass shattering below. Rachel climbs out the window.)*

TOM. Go! He won't see you! Stay in the dark! Keep in the shadows!

Scene 2

Rachel at a pay phone in her robe and slippers. Snow.

RACHEL. Jeanette? Rachel. Merry Christmas.... No, everything's great, but listen, would you and Freddie mind taking a little spin down here to the Arco station at Route 3 and Carl Bluestein Boulevard? No, no, nothing like that, I just came outside.... Oh, isn't it? It's beautiful, uh-huh, listen, Jeanette, Tom took a ... Tom.... It's so ridiculous. He took a contract out on my life.... A contract?... Uh-huh. Right. And, I mean, the man broke in downstairs so I thought I'd better go out of the house, so I climbed out over the garage and I was afraid to ring your bell because you have all those pretty lights and I was afraid he might be following my tracks in the snow — *(Lloyd approaches in the darkness.)* — and so I thought maybe you'd just zip down here and we'd all have some eggnog or something, what do you say?... Jeane — ? No.... No, I know, I am, I'm a kidder.... But — Merry Christmas to you too, Jeanette, please don't ... *(Jeanette has hung up. Rachel turns, sees Lloyd, screams.)* AAAA-AAAGH! NO, MY GOD! PLEASE!

LLOYD. *(Overlapping her, backing up.)* Hey. Hey.

RACHEL. Oh, I'm sorry. Did you want to use the phone? Please, go right ahead.

LLOYD. I'm just trying to find a gas station.

RACHEL. This is a gas station, right here, you found one. For *gas!* Oh, not on Christmas Eve, maybe up on the turnpike ... Merry Christmas.

LLOYD. Merry Christmas. You need a lift?

RACHEL. No. Yes. No.

LLOYD. It's no problem.

RACHEL. No. Thank you

LLOYD. You're sure?

RACHEL. No, thank you. I mean, yes — I....

LLOYD. Come on, hop in.

Scene 3

In the car.

RACHEL. Thank you.

LLOYD. Better?

RACHEL. Yes.

LLOYD. Where you headed?... Some night.

RACHEL. Yes. Yes. Christmas. I love Christmas.

LLOYD. Yeah.

RACHEL. Snow.... You have a family?

LLOYD.   No. Well, you know.... You?

RACHEL.   No.... No, no. *(Her wedding ring.)* Oh this? This is just costume. I just wear this, see? *(Tosses the ring out the window.)* Good-bye! That felt wonderful. Maybe you should just let me off up at the, uh.... Well, I can get off anywhere. Oh, you wanted to get gas. Where do you live?

LLOYD.   Springfield.

RACHEL.   Springfield.... The field of spring.

LLOYD.   You and your husband have a fight or something?

RACHEL.   I'm not married. You married?... You have a girl-friend.

LLOYD.   Just Pooty.

RACHEL.   Pooty ... Pooty.... My son does the cutest thing. I was married before. He's four and a half. My son has custody — my father — oh God. My son is four and a half, my husband has custody, my father is dead. And he does this thing — there are two boys, but Jeremy's just three. But Tom — Tom Junior, not my husband, Tom Senior — Tom Junior is always firing everybody, you know, if he doesn't like what you're doing. He'll say to his babysitter who is usually my friend Jeanette who can't have kids of her own because of this thing in her — uterus — he'll say to Jeanette, you know, um, "You're fired, Jeanette!" You know? Just because she wants to put him to bed or some-thing. And just today he fired me. I mean, on Christmas Eve. I said, "You're gonna fire your own mother?" "That's right," he said, "you're fired!" So.

LLOYD.   Now you're fired.

RACHEL.   Now I'm fired. What does Pooty do? Is that her name?

LLOYD.   Pooty.

RACHEL.   What does she do?

LLOYD.   She works.

RACHEL.   Oh, that's good. Do you work? *(He nods.)* Same place Pooty works? *(He nods.)* Now how did I know that? Not me, I've never worked. *(Pause.)* Did you tell me your name?

LLOYD.   Lloyd.

RACHEL.   Lloyd.

LLOYD.   Bophtelophti.

11

RACHEL. Bophtelophti. Isn't *that* an interesting name. I'm —
Mary Ellen Sissle. Is my maiden name.

LLOYD. Nice to meet you.

RACHEL. Don't let go of the wheel! Nice to meet you, too.
My father always said, "Don't interfere with the driver whilst
the vehicle is in motion." You think I'm escaped from an insti-
tution, don't you?

LLOYD. Are you? *(She laughs.)* What's so funny?

RACHEL. Nothing, I'm sorry, I just suddenly saw ... I mean,
me in my housedress and my slippers out in the snow.

LLOYD. Oh, it's cool.

RACHEL. Yes, it was. I've always wanted to do something like
that, you know? Run away in the middle of the night in your
slip and your slippers with some strange man who would ruin
your reputation and disappoint your parents terribly and disappoint your friends and just make you really happy. Well, I
think we get these ideas from rock-and-roll songs, actually.

LLOYD. Right.

RACHEL. Which is why I would never really do anything like
that except here I am. But, no, I mean, this isn't really like that,
I just meant running away and becoming.... Well, I don't know
what I thought I'd become. But running away. And here I am.

LLOYD. Here you are.

RACHEL. On my way to....

LLOYD. Meet Pooty.

RACHEL. Meet Pooty ... *(Pause.)* Lloyd?

LLOYD. Yeah?

RACHEL. Do you think we ever really know people? I mean,
I know we know people....

LLOYD. You mean really.

RACHEL. But really.

LLOYD. You mean *know* them.

RACHEL. Do you think?

LLOYD. Well ... I don't know.

RACHEL. I don't know either. I mean, I suppose I know lots
of people.

LLOYD. Sure you do.

RACHEL. And you know lots of people.

LLOYD. Pooty.

RACHEL. We live our lives and we know lots of people and ... I don't know what I'm saying. D'you get a Christmas tree? *(He nods.)* That's nice. "Oh, Christmas tree! Oh, Christmas tree ..." *(She stops singing, near tears.)*

LLOYD. It's all right.

RACHEL. I know....

LLOYD. The holidays can be tough sometimes.... You see your parents?

RACHEL. Not since they died....

LLOYD. You'll spend Christmas with us.

Scene 4

Living room.

RACHEL. Don't wake her.

LLOYD. Oh, she'll be glad to meet you. *(He goes off.)*

RACHEL. I love your house.... Be calm....

LLOYD. *(Back.)* She'll be out in a sec.

RACHEL. This is so Christmasy.

LLOYD. How 'bout a rum toddy?... Comin' right up! *(He goes off again.)*

RACHEL. This is so lovely....

LLOYD. *(From off.)* Glad to have the company. *(Pooty enters in her wheelchair.)*

RACHEL. Surprise! Hello, Rachel — Mary Ellen! Rachel Mary Ellen, the Rachel is silent. Nice to meet you. This is so nice. I hope I'm not, you know. I feel.... Well, actually, my house burned down and Lloyd was kind enough to say I could stop in. You know, stop up. So, I'm, uh, not.... *(No reaction. Lloyd returns.)*

LLOYD. You have to keep your face towards her so she can read your lips

RACHEL. Oh, she's deaf. You're deaf! I'm sorry, not that you're deaf, but ... I just *love* your house. *(Lloyd signs for Pooty.)*

LLOYD. The one and only Pooty-Poot-Pooter.

RACHEL. Yessssss.

LLOYD. *(Spelling her name.)* Mary Ellen Sizzler.

RACHEL. Well. Did you slip on the ice, it looks like.

LLOYD. She's paraplegic.

RACHEL. Paraplegic! Oh, paraplegic.

LLOYD. Paraplegic.

RACHEL. I have to keep my face this way, don't I?... Um....
Tell me, Pooty —

LLOYD. I'm just gonna check on the toddies. *(He goes out
again.)*

RACHEL. What kind of name is that? Your name. It's so unusual. *Your name! (Pooty jots on a piece of paper; Rachel reads.)*
"Pooty." Uh-huh. You know, I was just saying before.... *(Lloyd returns with two glasses.)*

LLOYD. She talk your ear off?

RACHEL. Thank you.

LLOYD. Pooter Bear.

RACHEL. Aren't you having any?

LLOYD. Never touch the stuff. Cheers.

RACHEL. Cheers. Sure there isn't any poison in here? *(She
smiles, drinks. Lloyd and Pooty confer in sign.)* Mmmmm.... Isn't
that beautiful the way you do that?

LLOYD. All right, everybody, have a seat. Time to open presents.

RACHEL. I'll watch. This'll be fun.

LLOYD. *(Handing her a gift.)* Merry Christmas. From us. Open
it.

RACHEL. But I didn't get anybody anything.

LLOYD. Go on.

RACHEL. Oh, I think this was meant for someone else. This
is so strange. *(Opens the package; it's a Shower Massage.)* Look!
Aren't you both so nice? Thank you.

LLOYD. You like it?

RACHEL. Ohhh, *like* it?

LLOYD. Okay, who's next?

RACHEL. Wait, okay, I know what I want to do. Now I'm sorry
I didn't get a chance to wrap this, but ... *(Gives Pooty her neck-
lace.)* Merry Christmas! Isn't this fun? I'll put it on.

LLOYD.   She says you didn't have to do that.

RACHEL.   Of course I didn't have to do that. You didn't have to ask a woman in her slippers to come spend Christmas with you either. I could be a mass killer. I could be anybody ... I could be anybody.

Scene 5

RACHEL.   *(On the telephone.)* Jeanette? Yes, Happy New Year, how are you? I'm great. So how was your Christmas, what did you get?... What? Oh, right now? Oh, I'm just up at my cousin's, you know. Of course I have a cousin, what do you mean you didn't know I had a cousin? Everybody has cousins. Where? I don't know, Jeanette, right up route — what difference does it make? But —.... No, I'm fine. Jeanette. Do I sound fine? Do I sound fine? Well. Oh shoot, here comes my bus, but listen do me a favor? No, I will, but — I can't Jeanette, but would you look in on the boys for me? When you get a chance? You will? Thanks, but listen, they're closing the doors, I've got to go. Okay. Bye, Jeanette! *(She hangs up.)*

Scene 6

Living room.

LLOYD.   Earth to Mary Ellen?

RACHEL.   Hm?

LLOYD.   Hungry?

RACHEL.   No, thanks. Oh, I'll cook, how's that? What would you like?

LLOYD.   What do you make?

RACHEL.   Whatever you want, just name it. It's yours.

LLOYD.   Whatever we want?

RACHEL.   Whatever you want.

LLOYD.   *(After conferring in sign with Pooty.)* Well we've discussed it.

RACHEL.   Uh-huh?

LLOYD.   And we both want you to stay here.

RACHEL.   For dinner?

LLOYD.   For as long as you like.

RACHEL.   Oh no, I couldn't.

LLOYD.   Why?

RACHEL.   Well, I mean, I could, but I can't.

LLOYD.   Well?

RACHEL.   No. Thank you, though. Very much.

LLOYD.   Why can't you?

RACHEL.   Because.

LLOYD.   Because why?

RACHEL.   Because.

LLOYD.   Because why?

RACHEL.   Lloyd.

LLOYD.   I'm serious

RACHEL.   Because I have to get a job, I have to get some shoes, I can't just move in. *(Pooty exits.)*

LLOYD.   Why not?

RACHEL.   Pooty, come on!

LLOYD.   She can't hear you, she's deaf.

RACHEL.   Thank you, Lloyd, I'm having enough trouble as it is.

LLOYD.   Well?

RACHEL.   Because.

LLOYD.   Because why?

RACHEL.   This is the way children talk.

LLOYD.   So?

RACHEL.   So? So's your old man. Just because. *(Pooty returns with her lap filled with shoes.)* And what is this? Shoes. Oh God, I love you both so much, I do. Why are you doing this?

LLOYD.   Because.

RACHEL.   And where *are* we, anyway? Where is Springfield?

LLOYD.   We've got an atlas.

RACHEL.   I mean, do you people even have identification? My mother may not even let me play with you. She's very fussy, you know. *(Lloyd opens the atlas.)*

LLOYD.   Here.... Hold on....

16

RACHEL. I believe you.

LLOYD. Springfield. If you lived here you'd he home by now.

RACHEL. *(Holding the book.)* Look how big the world is: it's all in this book.... Oh Lloyd ... I would love to stay here, you know that I would love to start my whole life right here at this second.

LLOYD. Why can't you?

RACHEL. Because. I'd have to get a job.

Scene 7

The office. Trish at a computer terminal. Roy and Rachel standing.

ROY. Hands Across the Sea is a not-for-profit, humanitarian foundation.

RACHEL. *(To Trish.)* Hi.

ROY. This does not mean we get away with murder.

RACHEL. Uh-huh.

ROY. Any of us. We all work very long, very hard hours for very little pay. Trish Hammers, this is our new clerk, Mary Ellen Sissle.

RACHEL. How do you do?

ROY. Americans lead soft, sheltered lives, I'm sure I don't need to tell you.

RACHEL. No.

ROY. We are barely cognizant of the human misery as it exists on this planet today, under our very noses too.

RACHEL. Really.

ROY. If I could pay you less than minimum wage, I would, believe me. Medical research, building a school in a foreign desert with illiterate, unskilled, underfed ignoramuses.... Well, it's expensive. Clinics, halfway houses, physical therapy labs where Lloyd and Pooty work —

RACHEL. Right.

ROY. Adult education programs, drug rehabilitation.... These are your insurance forms. Fill these out and give them to Mr.

17

Seakins. Then ask Trish for some documents to process, she'll explain how you do that. Any other questions come straight to me.

RACHEL. Great.

ROY. So, enjoy.

RACHEL. I will, thanks.

ROY. Welcome aboard.

RACHEL. Thank you. *(He goes out.)* He seems nice. *(She sits; her chair collapses.)* Whoops! I'm going to need insurance. Do you know how I, uh...? *(No response.)* Never mind, I got it. *(Adjusts seat.)* So how was your Christmas? You see your family?

TRISH. I'm not a big fan of Christmas.

RACHEL. Oh. Parents put coal in your stocking one year or something?

TRISH. My parents were killed when I was six months old.

RACHEL. Oh, I'm terribly sorry.

TRISH. Why? You didn't do it.

RACHEL. No, I know. *(Realizing her chair has sunk down again.)* Oh, God, I thought I was getting shorter. Is there another chair, do you know?... This is fine. *(Starts to fill in forms.)* Who's Mistress Eakins? I'm sorry, I'm supposed to take this to Mistress Eakins, do you know where she is?... Mistress Eakins? Do you know what I'm talking about?

TRISH. No.

RACHEL. Mistress Eakins, I think he said.

TRISH. Mr. Seakins.

RACHEL. Oh. I thought he said Mistress Eakins. I thought that was kind of a strange name, but mine is not to reason why, mine is just.... So where is he? Mr. Seakins.

TRISH. I'll give it to him.

RACHEL. No, I don't mind. *(Trish takes the forms from her.)* Well. So do you have any kids or anything?

TRISH. No.

RACHEL. No family?

TRISH. Nope.

RACHEL. Brothers and sisters? *(Trish shakes her head.)* Wow, you get your own screen and everything, huh?

TRISH. All right. I'd like you to take the white sheets, transfer everything onto the green sheets and staple them together. File everything in alpha-numerical order in the cabinets marked "Hardcopy." After that we'll go through the storeroom and if there's time I'll show you where the microfilm records are kept.

RACHEL.   Great.

Scene 8

Living room.

LLOYD.   So how was it?

RACHEL.   *(Signing to Pooty throughout.)* It was great.

LLOYD.   You liked Trish?

RACHEL.   Oh, yeah. Now she's in charge of what again?

LLOYD.   All the budget.

RACHEL.   Oh.

LLOYD.   And she's pretty convinced she doesn't need an assistant, either.

RACHEL.   Oh, really? Well.

LLOYD.   She'll loosen up.

RACHEL.   *(To Pooty.)* So then she does the payroll?... How do you say payroll, Lloyd?

LLOYD.   I don't know, ask her.

RACHEL.   No, come on.

LLOYD.   Spell it. I'll be out in the woodshed if anybody needs me.

RACHEL.   You're just trying to turn me into a deaf girl, I know.

LLOYD.   *(As he exits.)* I can't hear you! *(Rachel and Pooty sign for a moment.)*

RACHEL.   She does. She seems kind of tight-lipped.

POOTY.   She is. Now, listen, he can't know. *(Rachel is dumbfounded.)* It would break his heart ... I'm sorry I didn't say anything before.

RACHEL.   Oh, listen ... you know.

POOTY.   When I lost the use of my legs a friend drove me up here to Springfield to take a look at this place where they

19

worked with the handicapped. I watched the physical therapists working with the patients and there was one: I remember he was working with a quadriplegic. I thought he was the most beautiful man I'd ever seen. A light shining out through his skin. And I thought if I couldn't be with him I'd die. But I knew I would just be one more crippled dame as far as he was concerned, so my friend helped to get me registered as deaf and disabled. I used to teach sign language to the hearing impaired. I thought if I were somehow needier than the rest I would get special attention. I realized soon enough: everyone gets special attention where Lloyd is concerned. But by then it was too late. He was in love with me, with my honesty. He learned to sign; he told me how he'd run away from a bad marriage and changed his name so he wouldn't have to pay child support. He got me a job at Hands Across the Sea and I couldn't bring myself to tell him that I had another name and another life, that I'd run away too, because I owed the government so much money and wasn't able to pay after the accident. I believe in honesty. I believe in total honesty. And I need him and he needs me to be the person he thinks I am and I am that person, I really am that person. I'm a crippled deaf girl, short and stout. Here is my wheelchair, here is my mouth.

RACHEL. I'm not judging you.

POOTY. When he goes out I babble. I recite poetry I remember from grade school. I talk back to the television. I even call people on the phone and say it's a wrong number just to have a conversation. I'm afraid I'm going to open my mouth to scream one day and…. *(She does; no sound. Lloyd returns with fresh-chopped kindling.)*

LLOYD. Keep it down in here. How's it going?

RACHEL. Great. It's pretty good.

LLOYD. I'm sorry, I didn't hear you.

RACHEL. It's pretty good, I say.

LLOYD. I still can't hear you.

RACHEL. I said it's —

LLOYD. *WHAT?*

RACHEL. Oh. *(She signs. He signs and goes out again.)*

POOTY. He was the first person who ever heard me. Really

heard me. And I never had to make a sound. You mustn't ever tell him.

RACHEL.   I won't. I think people who love each other, whatever way they love each other, nobody should say it's right or wrong. *(Pause.)* Do you think Lloyd...? I mean, do you think he would ever ... hurt you? I mean, not hurt you, but....

POOTY.   Want to?

RACHEL.   Want to, say.

POOTY.   Sure. It wouldn't be love, would it?

RACHEL.   Would it?

POOTY.   Why?

RACHEL.   Oh, I don't know.

POOTY.   Did someone try to hurt you?

RACHEL.   Oh, no, no, no, no.

POOTY.   Who tried to hurt you?

RACHEL.   Nobody.

POOTY.   You can tell me.

RACHEL.   Tom wouldn't do anything like that. He wouldn't.

POOTY.   Who's Tom?

RACHEL.   *(Overlapping.)* Forget I mentioned it. Really. *(Beat.)*

POOTY.   I think you should talk to someone about this, don't you?

Scene 9

Doctor's office.

FIRST DOCTOR.   Go on.

RACHEL.   Well, I don't know. There's really no problem.

FIRST DOCTOR.   No?

RACHEL.   No. I don't know....

FIRST DOCTOR.   What are you thinking?

RACHEL.   I don't know. About Christmas, I guess.

FIRST DOCTOR.   Do you feel like telling me about it?

RACHEL.   Well, last Christmas? Christmas Eve? My husband Tom is all tucked into bed like a little kid and our two boys are in their beds, I've just tucked them in, and I tell Tom how per-

fect it all seems, I've never been so happy, which is true. And....
Well, my father was allergic to dogs, you know, and Tom didn't
like puppies, so I never said anything about wanting a puppy,
but I was thinking about it. And I was looking out into the snow
and talking about Alaska or something, but I was thinking
about how people in books and movies are always getting puppies on Christmas and you never see anybody having to clean
up the....

FIRST DOCTOR. Shit.

RACHEL. Or get hit by cars. You always see them with a big
red bow and the kids are smiling and — but I didn't say anything, I was just thinking it. I didn't want Tom to feel guilty if
he hadn't gotten me a puppy which I knew he hadn't because
he hates them, so it was just a private little something I was
thinking about and that's all I needed really was to think about
it and rub its little imaginary ears. And we were watching the
news, I remember, and suddenly I realize Tom's upset. So nat-
urally I assume he knows I really want a puppy, so I go to comfort him, because I don't care about it, really, if it's going to
make him unhappy, I don't even mention it, I just give him a
big hug and tell him it's Christmas and be happy and he says
he's taken a contract out on my life.

FIRST DOCTOR. This upset you.

RACHEL. Maybe I'm overreacting. Or he's kidding which I
think he must be. But anyway, I wind up spending Christmas
with this man I meet at the Arco station and his girlfriend who
is crippled and deaf, she says, you know, with hand signals until
suddenly she just turns to me and starts saying how she had to
pretend she was deaf to get the attention of this man we're all
living with who's changed his name and run away and she's
changed her name and I've changed my name and we're all
working in the same place and she's telling me all these secrets
and all of a sudden she says, "Why don't you talk to a psychia-
trist?"

FIRST DOCTOR. And here you are.

RACHEL. Here I am.

FIRST DOCTOR. When did you have this dream?

22

Scene 10

The office.

TRISH. I'm going to have to take an early lunch today, Mary Ellen.

RACHEL. Okay.

TRISH. So if you'll hold down the fort.

RACHEL. Anything I can do for you on the computer or anything?

TRISH. No, thanks.

RACHEL. Well, anytime you want to teach me.

TRISH. I think you probably have enough work to keep you busy. *(Trish goes out. Rachel looks around then moves over to Trish's seat. Lloyd enters.)*

LLOYD. Hi.

RACHEL. Hi

LLOYD. Mind if I join you?

RACHEL. No. Have a seat.

LLOYD. Learning Lotus?

RACHEL. No, what's that?

LLOYD. Oh, that's the software.

RACHEL. What's software?

LLOYD. Oh, that's what tells the computer what to do.

RACHEL. Oh.

LLOYD. I don't even know if that's what we use.

RACHEL. You know? In all the months I've been here Trish has never shown me how to do anything except file and take care of the storeroom and stuff like that

LLOYD. Well, give her time.

RACHEL. Yeah. I guess. She has no family.

LLOYD. Yeah.

RACHEL. She says.

LLOYD. What do you mean?

RACHEL. I don't know. Just for all we know she could have ten families and a trail of broken hearts behind her, right?

Who knows?

LLOYD. What else have you and Pooty been discussing?

RACHEL. Nothing.

LLOYD. Anything you'd like to ask me personally?

RACHEL. Oh, I wasn't even thinking about that.

LLOYD. Yes, I left my family. No, they don't know where I am —

RACHEL. No, I wasn't asking any of this.

LLOYD. *(Overlapping.)* No, I don't pay child support, no, Bophtelophti is not my real name —

RACHEL. Please, Lloyd.

LLOYD. My real name is Boyd T. Theophillo....

RACHEL. The past is irrelevant. It's something you wake up from.

LLOYD. I walked out on a woman with multiple sclerosis and two children, one of them brain-damaged, because I was too drunk to see him playing in the snow and I ran over him with the snow blower. I left them with no money and no way to feed themselves, moved as far away as I possibly could, changed my name, took the cash I'd stolen from the savings account to pay for the kids' education and put myself through school, so that I could become a physical therapist and work with multiple sclerosis victims and the occasional brain-damaged child with resultant motor-skill difficulties, none of whom held the slightest interest for me other than to remind me of what I could never escape as long as I live. And let's see. I married a nice crippled, deaf girl and I don't drink anymore. The past is something you wake up to. It's the nightmare you wake up to every day.

RACHEL. Well, these things happen for a reason, I believe that, I'm sorry, I do. And you're not helping anybody by punishing yourself. Why don't you pay back the money and say you're sorry?

LLOYD. It was thirty-five thousand dollars.

RACHEL. So? Big deal. People win that on game shows.

Scene 11

TV studio.

ANNOUNCER. And here's your host, Tim Timko!

TIM.   Okay, here we go, how does this game work, where are we? Oh, yes, it all comes back to me, like last night, who was that girl? Okay, enough of that, it's good to be back, let's see who's here. *(Houselights.)* Remember, all you need's a mother, a wife, and the crazy idea that you could tell the difference. Looks like an awful lot of bag ladies slipped in here. How're we all doin'? *(Crowd response.)* Anybody want to play this thing? What's it called? Your Brother's Wife? Your Sister's Best Friend's Mother-in-Law? *(Sign lights up. Rachel, Lloyd and Pooty are in the audience, dressed as the solar system with cardboard and paper-maché constructions over their heads.)* Your Mother Or Your Wife?! Ah! Wait. *(He makes his way over to the oddly costumed trio.)* Wait, wait a minute, I know what I like and don't tell me now, you folks are dressed as the solar system, aren't you?

LLOYD.   That's right, Tim.

TIM.   This looks like the planet Earth down here.

LLOYD.   That's my mother, Tim.

TIM.   Mother Earth.

LLOYD.   Right.

TIM.   I bet your world revolves around your sun, too, doesn't it. What's your name, sir?

LLOYD.   Lloyd.

TIM.   You have a last name, Lloyd?

LLOYD.   Bophtelophti.

TIM.   Where you from, Lloyd?

LLOYD.   Springfield?

TIM.   Springfield? Massachusetts? *(To Rachel.)* And you must be the little lady.

LLOYD.   That's right, Tim.

RACHEL.   Venus.

TIM.   Ah. "One touch of."

LLOYD.   That's right.

TIM.   Well, you've met our requirements, Lloyd.

LLOYD.   I should tell you, Tim, my mother is deaf. But my wife speaks sign language.

TIM.   So she can translate. Okay. Come on up and get set to play *Your Mother Or Your Wife! (Music, applause. Lloyd, Rachel and Pooty are led onstage.)* All right, correctly identify which of these lovely ladies answered each of three scintillating questions supplied by our studio audience made up entirely of Nobel Prize Laureates by the way — *(To someone in the audience.)* what, you don't believe me? Get him out of here. And you can win yourself up to twenty thousand dollars, Lloyd, and a chance to play for our grand prize.

ANNOUNCER.   Tim, the Bophtelophtis will be playing for a grand cash total of one hundred thousand dollars.

TIM.   A hundred grand. Are you ready for our glass booth?

LLOYD.   I guess so, Tim.

TIM.   Then take him away. *(Lloyd is led offstage.)* Never to be heard from again. *(To Rachel and Pooty.)* Good evening, ladies.

RACHEL.   It's great to be here, Tim!

TIM.   You're going to translate.

RACHEL.   That's right.

TIM.   No funny business. Anybody here speaks deaf, keep an eye on these two. All right, Venus, first question.

RACHEL.   Okay.

TIM.   Would you say that Lloyd is more like a Ping-Pong ball or a paper clip? Mmmmmm.

RACHEL.   I'll say a Ping-Pong ball.

TIM.   Any particular reason?

RACHEL.   He bounces around a lot?

TIM.   He does? Okay. Mom? Is Lloyd more like a Ping-Pong ball or a paper clip, would you say? Two Ps … *(Rachel and Pooty confer in sign.)*

RACHEL.   She says a paper clip.

TIM.   Because?

RACHEL.   Because he holds the family together.

TIM.   Awww, that's — disgusting. No, I'm just teasing you. Question number two: Mom first this time. If Lloyd were a salad dressing, what flavor would he be? If blank were a salad dressing....

RACHEL. She says blue cheese.

TIM. He's getting a little moldy? But okay, Venus?

RACHEL. I'll say blue cheese.

TIM. Blue cheese it is. Ladies, third question: If you could choose between your husband leaving you for another woman or, in Mom's case her son leaving her for another mom...? *(Looks to the control booth.)* Guys, this question doesn't make sense. What's he gonna do, get another mother?... Judges say fly with it. All right — between your husband leaving you for another woman or staying together, knowing he doesn't love you, Venus, which would it be?...

RACHEL. I'd have to say another woman.

TIM. Another woman. Mom? Between losing your son to another mother or knowing he didn't love you. All right, fair enough.

RACHEL. She says another mother.

TIM. "M" is for the many ways. Ladies, for our grand prize: Who does Lloyd love most, you or Mom?

RACHEL. His mother.

TIM. And Mom? This should be interesting. *(Rachel and Pooty confer. Pooty points to Rachel.)* And she says you! Okay, we'll be right back with the three happy Boopy-Boppies after this word from the good folks at Nu-Soft. Don't go away. *(Lights change; Lloyd is escorted onstage.)*

ANNOUNCER. We're going right on. Ten seconds.

TIM. *(To Rachel.)* Say your name for me.

RACHEL. Bophtelophti.

TIM. Bophtelophti. *(Lights restore.)*

ANNOUNCER. Five, four, three.... Rolling.

TIM. And we're back with the Bophtelophtis from Springfield, Massachusetts. Bophtelophti, is that Polish?

RACHEL. Yes, T —

LLOYD. *(Simultaneously.)* No, well, it's —

RACHEL. It's....

LLOYD. Welsh, actually.

RACHEL. Welsh and Polish.

TIM. Welsh and Polish. How long've you been married?

LLOYD. Ten....

RACHEL. Years.

TIM. Ten years. Any kids so far?

LLOYD. No.

RACHEL. But....

LLOYD. We're hoping, Tim.

TIM. Well, good luck to you. Because you're gonna need it! Okay, here we go, round two, Lloyd, for five thousand dollars: When asked if you reminded them of a paper clip or a Ping-Pong ball, who said "paper clip" and I quote, "Because he holds the family together." Your mother or your wife.

LLOYD. Boy.... My mother? *(Rachel hops up and down and claps.)*

TIM. Right you are if you think you are, Lloyd.

LLOYD. Okay.

TIM. For ten thousand dollars, when asked what type of salad dressing you reminded them of, who said "blue cheese"? Your mother or your wife.

LLOYD. That's my favorite.

TIM. Nobody's interested in your personal life, Lloyd. No, take your time.

LLOYD. I'll say both.

TIM. Both it is for a quick ten grand! All right, for twenty thousand dollars and a chance to lose it all, Lloyd: Which ... wait, let me get this straight. Which of the women in your life said they would rather lose you to another woman, wife or mother as the case may be, than believe you to be unhappy in their home. Mother Earth or the Venus de Milo, Lloyd. Lose you to another woman....

LLOYD. Both?

TIM. Both it is! Congratulations, Lloyd Bophtelophti from Warsaw, Wales, you've just won twenty thousand dollars and a chance to go home before you ruin your marriage.

LLOYD. No, we want to keep going.

TIM. Remember, if you miss this one, we keep it all, Lloyd, but you do go away with a free home version of *Your Mother Or Your Wife.*

LLOYD. We'll play.

TIM. He says he'll play. All right, no eye contact now, no help from the studio audience please, Lloyd, for one hundred thousand dollars *in cash,* we asked your mother and your wife: Who does Lloyd love the most? Who said — keep breathing, Lloyd — you love your wife the most? Your mother, your wife or your mother *and* your wife, it could be both. Don't think too hard, Lloyd.... Your mother, your wife or your mother and your wife ... I'm sorry, we're running out of time, we'll have to have an answer, Lloyd.

LLOYD. My mother.

TIM. Your mother! *(Lights flash. Audience screams. Rachel, Lloyd and Pooty express their enthusiasm.)* For one hundred thousand dollars, Lloyd Bophtelophti from Springfield, you've said the magic word, take the money, be happy, this is Tim Timko saying good night we'll see you next week with your mother, your wife, your mistress, whoever else you got out there....

ANNOUNCER. *(Under.)* For tickets to *Your Mother Or Your Wife* write your name and address on a postcard and mail it to, *Your Mother Or Your Wife,* Box 1224, New Hope Station, New York, New York.... *(His voice fades.)*

INTERMISSION

ACT TWO

Scene 1

The office.

TRISH. How much?

RACHEL. A hundred thousand dollars.

TRISH. You're kidding.

RACHEL. I'm not.

TRISH. That's....

RACHEL. Incredible, isn't it?

TRISH. It's incredible.

RACHEL. It's incredible. And you know what the moral is?

TRISH. What's the moral?

RACHEL. You can't be afraid.

TRISH. No.

RACHEL. These things happen for a reason, I keep saying it. I mean, we're all so afraid to take chances and what have we got to lose? We're all going to be dead in a hundred years anyway.

TRISH. This is true. *(Pause.)*

RACHEL. Trish?

TRISH. Uh-huh?

RACHEL. Remember when I first came here?... Wow, it's almost a year ago now, isn't it?

TRISH. That's right.

RACHEL. You didn't really like me, did you?

TRISH. Oh.

RACHEL. No, come on, it's all right.

TRISH. Well. I don't always warm up to people right away.

RACHEL. Oh, I know. But I think it's also because you thought I just wasn't smart enough to handle anything very complicated, didn't you?

TRISH. No.

RACHEL. Well, I decided to take the bull by the horns any-

30

way, and I've sort of been teaching myself about the computer.
TRISH.   You have?
RACHEL.   When you go to lunch. Look. I got this book on Lotus and I learned how to call up the menu and the file directory and everything.
TRISH.   Great.
RACHEL.   And I even figured out about the separate accounts you have filed that don't appear on the main index. You know, like the one that's attached to the Christmas fund as a footnote.
TRISH.   How'd you figure that out?
RACHEL.   Well, I was just, you know — I was trying to figure out what the password was and I was playing around with anagrams and stuff and your name spells "shirt," I'm sure you know, because you used it for the footnote file.
TRISH.   Good for you.
RACHEL.   Yeah. My dad and I used to like to play word games and things when I was little.... Anyway.... You're not mad, are you?
TRISH.   No, why should I be mad?
RACHEL.   Oh, I don't know. Actually, some of the math doesn't add up either, but....

Scene 2

Doctor's office.

FIRST DOCTOR.   In the dream....
RACHEL.   Uh-huh.
FIRST DOCTOR.   You pretend to be the wife and Pooty ... Pooty?
RACHEL.   Right.
FIRST DOCTOR.   Pooty is an unusual name.
RACHEL.   Mm-*hm.*
FIRST DOCTOR.   Pooty pretends to be the mother. *(Pause.)* Do you think there's any significance to that?
RACHEL.   No. I mean, you can't go on the show unless you

31

have a mother and a wife. That's just the way the game works, and Lloyd doesn't have a mother, so —

FIRST DOCTOR.   But Pooty is the wife and you are not a member of the family at all, unless we say that you are the adopted child.

RACHEL.   Right. But Pooty's deaf. I mean, she's not, but it was just easier to make her seem like a mother since she wouldn't have to talk and she's in a wheelchair. And it worked. I mean, we won the money and Lloyd paid back his ex-wife, so....

FIRST DOCTOR.   I know you haven't wanted to talk about your parents, Rachel, and we agreed you don't have to until you feel you're ready. The loss of our parents is the greatest single trauma of our adult lives. But I also believe that our dreams are a way of telling ourselves what we think we mustn't know, our secret wishes and fears, written in code, but the secret is there.

RACHEL.   Like an anagram.

FIRST DOCTOR.   Right. *(Pause.)* Why do you think you picked *Your Mother Or Your Wife?*

RACHEL.   Oh, they picked us. I mean, we just sent in the postcard.

FIRST DOCTOR.   Whose dream are we discussing?

RACHEL.   Nobody's. I'm sorry I didn't say that before. I thought that was part of the therapy, to talk about everything like it was a dream. It's not a dream. I'm sorry, I was confused. Sorry. *(Pause.)*

FIRST DOCTOR.   Would you like to see another therapist?

RACHEL.   No.

FIRST DOCTOR.   Is that what you're telling me?

RACHEL.   Not at all.

FIRST DOCTOR.   There's nothing shameful in that. I won't be angry with you. Sometimes it's a good idea to shop around, try different types of therapies.

RACHEL.   I know.

FIRST DOCTOR.   I honestly think it's time, Rachel, that you try to think about what it is in the loss of your parents that is so difficult to share with me. *(Pause.)*

RACHEL.   My mother was run over by a school bus when I was

six. My father died of a heart attack the year I married Tom.

FIRST DOCTOR. Thank you, Rachel. *(Pause.)* Rachel? Did you ever wish — not really mean it — just wish that your mother would go away? Did you think that you were responsible for what happened?

RACHEL. She was run over by a school bus.

FIRST DOCTOR. And then what happened?

RACHEL. I lived with my father.

FIRST DOCTOR. Until you were how old?

RACHEL. Nineteen.

FIRST DOCTOR. And then?

RACHEL. I married Tom.

FIRST DOCTOR. And your father died.

RACHEL. Of a heart attack.

FIRST DOCTOR. What is a heart attack? Isn't it a broken heart?

Scene 3

Living room. Lloyd and Pooty are dressed as Santa and a reindeer.

LLOYD. Ho, ho, ho!

RACHEL. Wait. Okay. Before we open presents — I love it! — I just want to say something, both of you. A year ago when I first came here and you both took me in … that was probably the nicest thing anybody ever did for me. You've taught me the true spirit of giving and Christmas; you've made me part of your family, you know? And … you're just the best family that anybody could ever ask for. *(Doorbell.)*

LLOYD. Aw, who the hell is that? *(He opens the door. Tom stands there, holding a bottle of champagne and a large gift box.)*

TOM. Is Rachel Fitsimmons here?

LLOYD. No, I'm sorry, there's no one here by that —

TOM. Rachel? It's Tom.

RACHEL. Oh, hi, how've you been?

TOM. May I come in?

RACHEL. Sure. Oh sure. Lloyd, Tom — Tom, Lloyd.

LLOYD. How do you do?

RACHEL. Lloyd, Pooty — Pooty ... Tom.

TOM. *(Indicating the champagne.)* This was, um, I found this sitting on the step. It says, "From Santa."

RACHEL. Uh-huh.

TOM. Nice to meet you all.

RACHEL. Pooty is deaf. And Tom is my husband.

TOM. How've you been, Rache?

RACHEL. Great. You?

TOM. I saw you on TV.

RACHEL. Uh-huh.

TOM. I almost didn't recognize you.

RACHEL. Oh.

TOM. You had a....

RACHEL. Planet.

TOM. On your....

RACHEL. Face.

TOM. Right. I thought maybe you'd remarried.

RACHEL. No.

TOM. That was....

RACHEL. Pretend.

TOM. TV. Right. *(Pause. He indicates gift box.)* I brought you something.

RACHEL. Oh.

TOM. It's something you've always wanted. And I'm sorry I didn't give it to you before. There isn't anything I can say, Rache. I keep trying to find the right words. Something that could make ... take away.... Take it away. It. There, you see, all I have to do is say it and there it is. What I did. The thing I can't ever take back. It. I can't live without you, Rache. And I can't live with — with it. I can't, but I'm just so afraid to die, Rachel, I'm afraid.

RACHEL. No one's going to die.

TOM. Well, we're all going to die.

RACHEL. Not right now, please.

TOM. I'm so sorry, Rachel.

RACHEL. Why don't we have some of this champagne? Lloyd,

would you get some glasses, please? *(Lloyd goes off.)* Oh Tom, it was very nice of you to bring the champagne, that means a lot to me.

TOM.   It was just sitting on the step.

RACHEL.   Oh, well, it was nice of someone then, wasn't it? *(To gift box.)* What's this? Is this for me?

TOM.   Uh-huh

RACHEL.   You brought this? I can't think what it could be.... Does anybody mind? *(Pooty signs. Rachel unwraps the package.)*

TOM.   The boys said if I brought you that maybe you'd come home. They're with Jeanette and Freddie for the weekend.

RACHEL.   Oh, how is Jeanette?

TOM.   Everybody sends their love. We all miss you.

RACHEL.   *(Looks in the box.)* Tom!

TOM.   You like him?

RACHEL.   Oh, he's so sweet.

TOM.   You can name him whatever you want.

RACHEL.   He's so beautiful. Look! Tom, thank you. *(She holds up a stuffed animal puppy.)*

TOM.   And you don't have to clean up after him.

RACHEL.   I know. Look, everybody!

LLOYD.   *(Returned with the champagne and a glass of milk for himself; he pours.)* Cute.

RACHEL.   Oh, thank you.

TOM.   You're welcome.

LLOYD.   How 'bout some champagne? Everybody like champagne? Poot? *(Hands them their glasses.)*

TOM.   Thanks.

RACHEL.   Awww.

LLOYD.   Drink up.

TOM.   Please come home, Rache. We miss you.

RACHEL.   Cheers! *(Clinks her glass against Tom's, over-emphatically, and her glass shatters.)* Whoops! Oh God.

LLOYD.   That's okay, I'll get you another one.

RACHEL.   Thanks. *(Lloyd goes off. To Tom and Pooty.)* Oh, go ahead, please. I'm fine.

TOM.   *(To Pooty.)* Cheers. *(Pooty signs the word for "cheers." She and Tom drink. Lloyd returns with another glass and pours.)*

LLOYD. Here you go.

RACHEL. Thank you, Lloyd. Cheers. *(Tom bends forward in sudden discomfort. Pooty emits a small noise.)*

TOM. Is there a bathroom?

LLOYD. Poot? *(Rachel holds her glass, untasted, watching as Tom and Pooty double over in pain.)*

TOM. Ow!

POOTY. Lloyd! *(Lloyd is stunned.)*

TOM. Jesus! Aaaagh!

POOTY. Lloyd!

TOM. Aaaaaaaa!

POOTY. AAAAAAAAAAAAAAAAAAA! *(They die.)*

Scene 4

The car. Rachel drives. Lloyd in his Santa suit.

RACHEL. Calm … calm…. Okay. Did I miss my exit? Okay. Lloyd? Okay. Okay, if we call the police — did we? Are we calling the police? Did we? No, I remember, okay. We could. Here's the thing: we didn't. We called the ambulance, okay. We called the ambulance. Why didn't we call the police? Because. They'll think we did it. Why will they think we did it? Because we didn't call the police. No, our fingerprints were on the bottle. "So what." "What do you mean 'So what?' Why did you leave your family? Why do you have assumed names? What are you hiding?" "Nothing." "Uh-huh. Where'd you get all this cash in hundred-dollar bills?" "Oh, we won it on a game show." "What game show?" *"Your Mother Or Your Wife."* "Is this your mother?" "No." "Is this your wife?" "No." Turnpike!… Is this the right ramp? Lloyd? *(Looks in rearview mirror.)* I think those people are following me. Are those the same people? No, wait, Tom brought the champagne! That's right, Tom brought the champagne. "We're all going to die," remember? *(She reads a road sign.)* West. We're all going to die. Just take a look over your shoulder and tell me if those are the same people…. No!

No, it was sitting on the step, that's right, remember? From Santa. Or he was lying. All right, wait. Wait. Maybe it was just a bad bottle. Maybe — maybe — they're following me. Don't turn around. Look like you're having a good time. Uh-huh! Uh-huh! Really!... Oh God. *(She turns on the radio.)*

ANNOUNCER.   The mellow sound of Nat King Cole. Gone before his time. It's ten A.M. Christmas morning. Let's hope Santa left something special under your tree. In the news — *(She turns off the radio.)*

RACHEL.   Wait a minute! Santa! Santa. Sat — na. At — sna. At — san. Tas — na. As — nat. Santa, Merry Christmas from Santa ... Sat — na. Sat — an. Satin. Satin. *Satan!* Merry Christmas from Satan! Oh God. Christ's birthday, Merry Christmas from Satan, Lloyd! That's horrible. Why is this happening? Why is it always Christmas? I love Christmas. I always used to say I wanted to live in Alaska because they had snow all year round and Santa was up there, so it must always be Christmas.... Oh Lloyd. They won't feel any more pain from now on, I know they won't. No more pain from now on, all right, Santa Claus? I'll drink to that.

Scene 5

Night. Snow. Rachel is still driving. Lloyd in his suit, staring.

RACHEL.   Toopy.... P.... Oop. Oopy. Toopy. Poot. Pyoot. Ypoot. Ytpoo. It. It ... Toopy. Two Ps. Two ... Y-po-to. Toy — po. Poy sounds like boy. Two boys! I have two boys. *(Pause.)* I don't even know what state we're in, do you? *(Sees road sign.)* Wait, can you read that?... Spring ... *field.* Springfield!?!? Is that what it said? How can we be back in Springfield — *(Reads.)* Ohio! Springfield, Ohio, thank you, God! Springfield, Ohio ... *(Sighs with relief.)* Oh God. Who would ever want to live in Springfield, Ohio? *(She has a revelation.) Nobody.*

37

Scene 6

A seedy hotel room; Lloyd remains in his Santa suit.

RACHEL.   Lloyd, I know we can be happy here, I just know we can. Who would ever think to look for us in Springfield, Ohio! Nobody. Why would we ever want to go back to Springfield? We wouldn't, you see, we wouldn't! And the lady at the real estate agency said there's one in every state. Fifty Springfields. So we don't have to stay here if we don't like it. We don't have to do anything. We can go anywhere, we can be anybody. We can go from Springfield to Springfield. How many people ever get a chance to do that in their whole lives?... Lloyd ... I know I can't take her place. But she'll always be right here. You're what keeps her memory alive. But you have to keep yourself alive. You have to *eat* something. And we have to get you out of that suit. We're lucky to be alive, I mean, we could have had some of that champagne. Well, you don't drink, but.... Let's pick names. What do you like? How about Jessie? I'll be Jessie or you be Jesse and I'll be Mrs. Mancini. I can find a new doctor. You know, it's a good idea to shop around, try different types of therapies —

LLOYD.   SHUT UP! SHUT THE FUCK UP PLEASE! COULD WE HAVE ONE — TINY — MOMENT OF SILENCE IF IT ISN'T TOO MUCH TO ASK FOR? PLEASE? *(Pause.)*

RACHEL.   I'm sorry.

LLOYD.   What?

RACHEL.   I said I'm sorry.

LLOYD.   I can't hear you. *(Pause.)*

RACHEL.   I said.... *(Pause. Rachel signs "I'm sorry.")*

Scene 7

Another Doctor's office.

SECOND DOCTOR.   Do you have nightmares, Mrs. Mancini?
RACHEL.   No.
SECOND DOCTOR.   Phobias?
RACHEL.   No.
SECOND DOCTOR.   Eczema? Asthma?
RACHEL.   No.
SECOND DOCTOR.   Do you take drugs?
RACHEL.   No.
SECOND DOCTOR.   Alcohol?
RACHEL.   No.
SECOND DOCTOR.   Are you an alcoholic?
RACHEL.   No.
SECOND DOCTOR.   Would you say you're chronically depressed?
RACHEL.   No.
SECOND DOCTOR.   Or unfulfilled in any way?
RACHEL.   No.
SECOND DOCTOR.   Have you ever tried to kill yourself?
RACHEL.   No.
SECOND DOCTOR.   Is it difficult for you to make a decision?
RACHEL.   No.
SECOND DOCTOR.   Are you sure?
RACHEL.   Mm-hm.
SECOND DOCTOR.   Do you have trouble sleeping?
RACHEL.   No.
SECOND DOCTOR.   You sleep too much?
RACHEL.   No.
SECOND DOCTOR.   Dietary difficulties?
RACHEL.   No.
SECOND DOCTOR.   Overeating?
RACHEL.   No.
SECOND DOCTOR.   Undereating?
RACHEL.   No.
SECOND DOCTOR.   Is sex a problem for you, Mrs. Mancini?

RACHEL. No.

SECOND DOCTOR. Does that embarrass you, my asking?

RACHEL. No.

SECOND DOCTOR. Do you ever have any trouble relating to new people?

RACHEL. No.

SECOND DOCTOR. Telling the truth?

RACHEL. No.

SECOND DOCTOR. No?... What's the problem?

RACHEL. My husband tried to kill me.

SECOND DOCTOR. Tried to kill you?

RACHEL. Twice.

SECOND DOCTOR. Why would he want to kill you?

RACHEL. I don't know.

SECOND DOCTOR. Did you call the police?

RACHEL. No.

SECOND DOCTOR. Why didn't you call the police?

RACHEL. Because I didn't think they'd believe me.

SECOND DOCTOR. Why wouldn't they believe you?

RACHEL. Because I'd run away and changed my name and was living with another man and his wife and then when they all got poisoned....

SECOND DOCTOR. Who got poisoned?

RACHEL. My husband and the other man's wife. Did. Pretty much.

Scene 8

Another hotel room.

LLOYD. You know what I feel like having?

RACHEL. What?

LLOYD. You know what I really feel like having?

RACHEL. What?

LLOYD. You know what I really feel like having right now?

RACHEL. What?

LLOYD. Champagne.

Scene 9

Another Doctor's office.

THIRD DOCTOR.   You're not from Alabama.
RACHEL.   No.
THIRD DOCTOR.   Now how did I know that?
RACHEL.   You see, two Christmases ago, my husband Tom.... Well, we've lived in Springfield before.
THIRD DOCTOR.   Oh, you have.
RACHEL.   Twice. And I have two sons, too, actually. And my husband tried to kill me twice, too.
THIRD DOCTOR.   Your husband? Tried —
RACHEL.   *(Overlapping.)* Two Ps!... Pooty.... My first shrink said that Pooty was a unusual name.
THIRD DOCTOR.   Oh, you've been in therapy before.
RACHEL.   Twice. But.... Okay: How long do you think a person could live if they drank nothing but champagne and they didn't eat anything? Just out of curiosity.
THIRD DOCTOR.   Well....
RACHEL.   Does a month seem like a long time? To you.

Scene 10

Another hotel room.

LLOYD.   Here's a question.
RACHEL.   No.
LLOYD.   Do you remember asking me if we ever really know anybody?
RACHEL.   Not until you eat something.
LLOYD.   You remember that?
RACHEL.   *(Unpacking groceries.)* Do you hear me?
LLOYD.   You asked me if I thought we ever really knew anybody.
RACHEL.   You are going to eat something if it kills me.
LLOYD.   And I've thought about it.... And I would have to

41

say....

RACHEL. You don't have to taste it.

LLOYD. My considered opinion would be....

RACHEL. Just smell it.

LLOYD. No. No way.

RACHEL. Croissants, Lloyd!

LLOYD. Not on your life.

RACHEL. Look, pâté.

LLOYD. No dice.

RACHEL. Just open your mouth and take one bite.

LLOYD. Ixnay.

RACHEL. Strawberries.

LLOYD. Nope.

RACHEL. Ice cream.

LLOYD. Uh-uh.

RACHEL. It's pistachio.

LLOYD. No way, Jose.

RACHEL. Lloyd, you can't —

LLOYD. Forget about it.

RACHEL. Soup. Soup!

LLOYD. No chance.

RACHEL. You can't survive on champagne alone, it's an old saying.

LLOYD. No, no, a thousand times no.

RACHEL. I need you now.

LLOYD. *Nyet.*

RACHEL. Please.

LLOYD. *Non.*

RACHEL You can't live on wine.

LLOYD. *Nein!*

Scene 11

Another Doctor's office.

FOURTH DOCTOR.   This is very important, Cheryl. We've talked about the birth scream. It's a terrible shock to be torn away in a shower of blood with your mother screaming and your home torn open and the strange doctor with his rubber hands slapping you with all his might and the cold light piercing the dark, the warm beautiful wet dark, the silent murmuring safe dark of Mummy everywhere and Daddy, everything is one and everything is sex and we are all together for eternity and we are happy and nothing ever passes through your mind but good thoughts until suddenly this squeezing is going on around you and everyone is pushing and pulling and cold steel tongs pinch your skin and pull you by the top of your head and you don't want to go, no, you don't want to leave your home where you're always floating and your mother's heart is always beating for something unknown and cruel where people are cold and you're stinging now, everything is breaking, it makes you want to scream, Cheryl, makes you want to scream the scream of all ages, scream of the greatest tragedy of all time and your mummy is screaming and your daddy is screaming and now all the doctors are screaming and everything's blinding you and you're torn away and they're hitting you and they throw you up in the air you open your eyes and your mother is covered in blood and you scream, Cheryl, scream, scream, *scream,* Cheryl, SCREAM, *SCREAM!!! (Pause.)* All right, we'll try it again.

Scene 12

Another Doctor's office and another hotel room.

LLOYD.   Not all champagne is champagne. They call it champagne. Sure, they call it champagne. I'll tell you what is interesting about champagne. Pain. It is pains-takingly made. They take great pains.

FIFTH DOCTOR.   Say I am a decent human being.

RACHEL.   I am a decent human being.

FIFTH DOCTOR.   Say I deserve to be loved.

RACHEL.   I deserve to be loved.

FIFTH DOCTOR.   Now repeat everything after me. I was put on this earth to love and be loved.

LLOYD.   Great pains, believe me.

FIFTH DOCTOR.   I was put on this earth....

RACHEL.   I was put on this earth to love and be loved....

FIFTH DOCTOR.   I am whole when I am alone and I am part of everything.

LLOYD.   *(Overlapping.)* And it is only in the region of Champagne where champagne is made.

FIFTH DOCTOR.   Mrs. Bophtelophti?... I said I am whole when I am alone and I am part of everything.

RACHEL.   Uh-huh.

FIFTH DOCTOR.   And I would like you to repeat that.

RACHEL.   Wait a minute.

FIFTH DOCTOR.   What?

RACHEL.   Wait a minute!

FIFTH DOCTOR.   What?

RACHEL.   You know what? Things just happen. People die. And bus drivers don't always look where they're going, even if they should, even if they're driving a school bus. Even if you love somebody they can still take a contract out on your life. And if you try to help somebody because they've been kind to you when you needed them, they can *still* refuse to eat and drink nothing but champagne, cham*pagne,* that's all they'll drink, and if you ask them to please, *please* take off their Santa

Claus suit, just when they go out, just when you go to the store, they won't. So? Things just happen!

Scene 13

Another hotel room. Lloyd moans in the glow of the television.

RACHEL. I'm here. Shhhh. I'm here, here we go. Mother's milk. *(Produces two bottles of champagne.)* It's your Christmas present, all right? I couldn't think what else to get you. I'm sorry. I got you two bottles. We're going to have a festive Christmas, just the two of us. It's our anniversary, too, remember? Don't you want to listen to the news?... Where's the knob? Did you pull out the knob? *(She takes the knob from him. He tries to remove a champagne cork, but is too weak.)* It's the one night in the year they save up all the good news. Don't you want to hear it? I'll help you with that, just a sec. Look. Doesn't the woman look like Trish Whatshername from Hands Across the Sea. Hammers. *(Putting in the knob.)* My God! Lloyd, look! *(Sounds come on.)*
ANNOUNCER. — refused to comment, but local spokesmen say Ms. Hammers may have embezzled as much as a half a million dollars in her more than twenty years as an accountant for the humanitarian organization.
RACHEL. *(Under.)* Oh my....
ANNOUNCER. David Harbinger spoke with Roy Morgrebi, president of the northeast chapter of Hands Across the Sea in Springfield.
RACHEL. There's Roy! Lloyd!
ROY. It just boggles the mind, you know. Very sweet girl.
SECOND ANNOUNCER. Would you say this is something we should all begin to be wary of? Donating money to charity —
ROY. No.
SECOND ANNOUNCER. — which will end up somehow in private hands?
ROY. Definitely not. I feel this is an isolated case, one hopes, and obviously we intend to institute tighter controls.

FIRST ANNOUNCER.   Police are still looking for the two alleged accomplices in last year's Christmas killing here in Springfield. More news after this word.

RACHEL.   *(Over the fading sound of a commercial.)* They think we did it! Lloyd! They think we did it.... She tried to poison us! And it wasn't Tom! It wasn't Tom at all!... Lloyd, we've got to go to the police, because WE DIDN'T DO IT! Don't you see? Okay! Okay! Say good-bye to Springfield! *(Lloyd is dead.)* Say good-bye.... *(He slumps forward. Rachel grabs him by the shirt, shakes him, lets him fall.)*

Scene 14

A shelter. Rachel, The Sixth Doctor and two derelicts in front of the television.

TV ANNOUNCER.   Street people they're called and Anne Lacher-Holden has the story.

FIRST DERELICT.   *(Overlapping.)* Shit on the floor, shit on the floor and you know it!

SIXTH DOCTOR.   *(Overlapping.)* This is us, don't you want to listen?

WOMAN ANNOUNCER.   In the summertime they seem to be everywhere, but where do they go in the winter? It is in shelters like this one, in storefronts all over the city where the needy, the cold and hungry, come for food and comfort. How many of these people would starve to death if not for the efforts and dedication of individuals like Dr. Mahalia Maden.

SECOND DERELICT.   Dr. M & M's!

WOMAN ANNOUNCER.   Doctor, how many years have you been running this shelter?

SIXTH DOCTOR'S VOICE.   Six years this Christmas, Anne.

WOMAN ANNOUNCER.   And where do you get your funds?

SECOND DERELICT.   *(Under.)* Steal it

SIXTH DOCTOR'S VOICE.   Well, money's a funny thing, you know. A lot of people want to help save the whales, but tell them they can help save a human being....

WOMAN ANNOUNCER.   That's right. What kind of people stay here and where do they come from?

SIXTH DOCTOR'S VOICE.   All over. We have bank presidents, writers, you name it.

WOMAN ANNOUNCER.   What brings them here?

SIXTH DOCTOR'S VOICE.   Life's been reckless with these people, Anne. Some more than others. Often they carry no identification whatsoever, it's difficult.

WOMAN ANNOUNCER.   I see.

SIXTH DOCTOR'S VOICE.   We have one of our people, I guess you could say she's our mascot. She came to us for our first night six years ago on Christmas Eve — no idea who she was, no name, we thought she was deaf. I'll be darned if a few weeks ago she didn't start to talk in her sleep. Talks a blue streak.

WOMAN ANNOUNCER.   Really?

SIXTH DOCTOR'S VOICE.   Who's to say these people can't lead normal, healthy lives again.

WOMAN ANNOUNCER.   You say they can. Doctor, it's been a pleasure talking with you. I'm Anne Lacher-Holden with *Street Beat*.

SECOND DERELICT.   I'm bored.

ANNOUNCER.   Thank you, Anne. Coming up we'll take a look at a woman who claims she's Santa Claus. And Marge von Bargen will — *(Sixth Doctor switches off the television.)*

FIRST DERELICT.   Shit on your floor and you know it! *(Derelicts disperse.)*

SIXTH DOCTOR.   *(To Rachel.)* No more secrets now, Eve. The whole world knows you can hear me and you know you hear me, because you spoke to me last night. Look at me: I asked you what was wrong and you said you were afraid and you were not asleep, Eve, so don't try that with me now. Your eyes were open and you answered me. Look at me: you answered me. What did you say? Everyone's afraid, Eve, I'm afraid. What did you say? A man in a ski mask who follows you when you leave here. Why does he follow you? Whose face is he hiding, Eve? Whose face? Behind the mask … I have bad dreams too, Eve. I wake up in the middle of the night, too, and want someone to hold me. I remember what I did to someone once and can never, never undo. Because you can never give back a life. But I made a pledge to myself that I would try. And I went to school and I studied to be a doctor and I swore to myself that I would scrimp and save and deny myself and do anything, Eve, if I could give one person back their life. And six years ago on Christmas Eve we opened the doors here. Who do you think was the first person to walk in off the street and join us? Eve.... Do you want to know my dream? That someday you'll trust me. And tell me all your dreams, all the good ones, so I can help you make them all come true. That's my dream.... The TV people gave me some tickets to a talk show. Would you like that? A talk show? How does that sound?

Scene 15

HOST.   And we're back with the author of *Unrepentant Killer.* Sue, if you hadn't been acquitted, do you think you'd still feel this same sense of —
SUE.   Yes —
HOST.   — purpose.
SUE.   My husband was able to terrorize me and —
HOST.   Uh-huh.
SUE.   — my kids because we were too frightened he might hurt *us.* But our rage was there, believe me.
HOST.   As was borne out by your — subsequen — ...
SUE.   *(Overlapping.)* Look out here at all these faces: these people are all potential killers — again, I'm not recommending they do what I did.
HOST.   Perhaps you wouldn't have had to —
SUE.   That's right.
HOST.   — if you'd felt —
SUE.   *(Overlapping slightly.)* *Experienced* my own fury, yes.
HOST.   *(Overlapping.)* Yes. Right.
SUE.   Here, see, now this right here is a perfect example of what I call the I-Am-Unworthy-Please-Oh-Who?-Me?-I-Wouldn't-Hurt-A-Fly type. *(Sue approaches the front row of the audience. Mon-*

itors reveal Rachel and Sixth Doctor seated. Sue addresses Rachel.) Stand up, please.

SIXTH DOCTOR.   No, she can't, really —

SUE.   Yes, she can, give her some credit — Come.

SIXTH DOCTOR.   No, really — *(To Rachel as she drags her C.)*

SUE.   I bet I know who you'd like to kill already. *(Turns Rachel to face the audience.)* There. Now isn't she lovely? *(Applause.)* Pick a face out there and imagine firing a bullet right between their eyes. Any one. Bam! Right between their beady little slits.... *(Rachel stares out blankly.)* See? She's terrified someone's going to hurt *her. (To Rachel.)* This time you're going to get *them.* Say "I am a cold-blooded killer. I, —" What's your name? *(Rachel has seen something in the audience.)* Do you have a name?

RACHEL.   No.

SIXTH DOCTOR.   Good, Eve!

SUE.   Eve, okay.

RACHEL.   No.

SUE.   "I, Eve, am a cold-blooded —"

RACHEL.   *(Overlapping "I, Eve —")* NOOOOOOOO! *(At the same time, a man in a ski mask has screamed from the aisle of the theatre.)*

MAN.   DEVIL WOMAN! *(He rushes the stage, pointing a handgun at Rachel.)*

HOST.   Look out! Somebody! *(The gun goes off. Rachel ducks and Sue, author of* Unrepentant Killer, *is mortally wounded. Pandemonium.)* Look out. My god! Doctor! DOCTOR!

RACHEL.   NO! NO! NO! NO! *(Host and Sue disappear. The Sixth Doctor has rushed to Rachel's side.)*

Scene 16

The action is continuous. Rachel repeats the word "no" over and over again, struggling to break free from the Sixth Doctor.

SIXTH DOCTOR.   Yes! Yes, Eve, yes! Look at me, yes, you spoke, yes, yes, yes. You spoke. Look at me. You spoke. Eve, yes, say yes. Say yes. Shhhh, I'm here, close your eyes, I'm here, yes you spoke. Yes, and I was wrong. There was a man. You were so right, there was a man and I was wrong, I'm sorry, Eve, I was wrong. There was a man and he was trying to hurt you, but he's gone now. *(Rachel has quieted down.)* We'll never know why he was trying to hurt you. The important thing is you spoke out loud and people heard you and I heard you and *you* heard you, Eve. You heard you. You. Eve. If you can tell yourself what you want, you can have it. I swear to you. I used to drive a school bus. Did you know that? I drove a school bus. And how many bus drivers do you think become doctors, Eve? None. Not at all. *Except the ones who do.* All right, Eve, close your eyes. I want you to imagine a place. I want you to imagine the most beautiful place in all the world. I don't want you to think about what anybody said you could or couldn't do. I want you to dream, Eve. I want you to imagine a time of year — your favorite time of year, the weather that gives you goosebumps — the right temperature, the right light in the sky, the right smell in the air. I want you to imagine someone standing there, Eve. Someone who makes people feel good about themselves and does all the things you ever wanted to do and has all the things you ever wanted to have. I want you to imagine that person standing there in that place at that exact time of day doing exactly what that person would be doing ... Eve ... if that person....

Scene 17

An office.

RACHEL.   Yes?
WOMAN PATIENT.   That's the end.
RACHEL.   You wake up?
WOMAN PATIENT.   I wake up.
RACHEL.   And how do you feel?
WOMAN PATIENT.   Happy.
RACHEL.   The dream makes you feel happy?
WOMAN PATIENT.   Yes.
RACHEL.   I'm afraid we're going to have to stop here, Sharon.
WOMAN PATIENT.   But what does it mean?

RACHEL. What does what mean?

WOMAN PATIENT. Why am I happy?

RACHEL. Does there have to be a reason?

WOMAN PATIENT. I don't know.

RACHEL. You're happy.

WOMAN PATIENT. Yes.

RACHEL. You feel happy now?

WOMAN PATIENT. Yes. Oh. That's what it means. It means I'm happy.

RACHEL. Yes.

WOMAN PATIENT. It means I'm happy.

RACHEL. It could mean that.

WOMAN PATIENT. It means I'm happy. Thank you.

RACHEL. Don't thank me, thank yourself.

WOMAN PATIENT. *(With Rachel.)* "Thank yourself." Well ... Merry Christmas.

RACHEL. You too, Sharon.

WOMAN PATIENT. I'll see you next week. *(She leaves.)*

RECEPTIONIST. *(Pokes her head in.)* Doctor, there's a student here from the University of Alaska waiting to see you. They called while you were in your session to say he was coming over.

RACHEL. Send him in, thanks.

RECEPTIONIST. *(To the offstage student.)* You can go on in. There you go. *(She exits as Tom Junior enters.)*

TOM JUNIOR. Doctor?

RACHEL. Yes, I'm — *(Her throat catches.)* Sorry, there's something caught in my throat. I'm sorry if I kept you waiting.

TOM JUNIOR. *(Extending his hand.)* Tom Fitsimmons.

RACHEL. Tom. Won't you, please.... Have a seat, Tom. Please. Anywhere. *(He sits in the only chair.)* What's the problem? What can I do for you? Take your time, relax, Tom, what's the story?

TOM JUNIOR. I, uh ... I was just trying to get some sleeping pill's and they said I would have to, uh....

RACHEL. I see.

TOM JUNIOR. You look really familiar.

RACHEL. I do?

TOM JUNIOR. You look really familiar. Where do I know you

51

from?...

RACHEL.   Why do you think you're having trouble sleeping, Tom? Are you? Having trouble?

TOM JUNIOR.   I know who you look like.

RACHEL.   Your mother.

TOM JUNIOR.   Yes.

RACHEL.   That's the transference, Tom. The patient projects an image onto the parent. Onto the....

TOM JUNIOR.   It's incredible.

RACHEL.   But you say you feel you need something, is that right?

TOM JUNIOR.   No, but like I've only seen pictures of her, but you really do. I mean, you're a lot older.

RACHEL.   Of course.

TOM JUNIOR.   But still, I mean, it's ... incredible.

RACHEL.   Good.... Tom, what is all this about sleeping pills? Is that what you need?

TOM JUNIOR.   Sort of.

RACHEL.   Why?

TOM JUNIOR.   I can't sleep. But I mean, it's just for this week. I mean, next week I'll be fine, so it doesn't have to be very many.

RACHEL.   Why is it just this week?

TOM JUNIOR.   Because.

RACHEL.   Does it have something to do with Christmas?...

TOM JUNIOR.   You know, I really feel better now that we've talked. I really do. I don't think I need sleeping pills at all, it's incredible, thank you.

RACHEL.   Sit down.

TOM JUNIOR.   I'm serious.

RACHEL.   Sit down, Tom. What is it about Christmas?... Some people think that the things you're afraid to think about are the things which eventually destroy you. And that if you talk about them, as painful as that is, it helps them to go away.

TOM JUNIOR.   I'm not afraid to think about them.

RACHEL.   Then what is it? You think I won't believe you?

TOM JUNIOR.   Maybe.

RACHEL.   Why don't you try me?

52

TOM JUNIOR. My mother.... The one....

RACHEL. Right.

TOM JUNIOR. Ran away like on Christmas.

RACHEL. How old were you?

TOM JUNIOR. Four.

RACHEL. Go on.

TOM JUNIOR. So the next year, our father, you know, leaves us with friends so — he says because he's going to bring our mother back, because ... I don't know.

RACHEL. You have brothers and sisters?

TOM JUNIOR. One brother. Younger. And instead he gets killed.

RACHEL. Your — ?

TOM JUNIOR. Father. By.... Well, it probably had something to do....

RACHEL. I'm listening.

TOM JUNIOR. It may have had something to do with this whole ... scandal. Anyway, he died. And they said our mother was involved, but they never were able to find her. And so we were raised, you know, by — my brother and I — by these neighbors and they were really nice. And then ... my brother disappeared when he was twelve and we didn't hear anything for a long time. And then he called and said he found this woman in California and she was gonna pay or something and ... I guess he just freaked out and he shot this lady on some talk show right around Christmas time.... I don't know. I mean, they didn't convict him, but ... I kind of thought I'd get away, you know? Alaska seemed like the place.

RACHEL. It is.

TOM JUNIOR. Not really. They have Christmas here too.

RACHEL. You have no memories of your mother, Tom?

TOM JUNIOR. No. Oh, yes, I do — one. But I mean, I think I dreamed it. I mean, I don't know. I think I dreamed it.

RACHEL. What is the memory?

TOM JUNIOR. Well, it's Christmas.

RACHEL. Uh-huh.

TOM JUNIOR. And, um, she's like reaching up, putting something up.

RACHEL.   On the tree.

TOM JUNIOR.   Uh-huh. Or something. And she's really ... she's really happy. Everything's bright and she's all in a glow and she looks right at me and says, "How's that?"

RACHEL.   "How's that?"

TOM JUNIOR.   Like that. And I don't know. I just said it, you know?

RACHEL.   What?

TOM JUNIOR.   Lousy, you're fired. I was just kidding.

RACHEL.   Of course.

TOM JUNIOR.   But ... sometimes it seems like that was the start of everything. It's like I hurt her feelings or something and she left and my father left and my brother left ... I keep feeling like if I could just go back to that — time. And she would turn to me, you know, all lit up and say, "How's that?" I'd say, "Beautiful, Mom." You know.

RACHEL.   Uh-huh.

TOM JUNIOR.   Because it was like for one second I wanted to spoil everything. Everybody was too happy and I was too excited. But I would take it back. I would take it all back, because I didn't mean it.

RACHEL.   Of course you didn't mean it.

TOM JUNIOR.   No, but I can't. It's like I can't wake up. I just know — I feel if I could just wake up, we'd all be there around the tree and my mom and dad would take care of me. And I keep pinching myself and pinching....

RACHEL.   Trying to wake up.

TOM JUNIOR.   Yes. I just keep wishing —

RACHEL.   Yes.

TOM JUNIOR.   — for....

RACHEL.   Someplace where it's always Christmas.

TOM JUNIOR.   Yes. How do you know?... Oh, I see, now you become my mother.

RACHEL.   How's this time for you, Tom? Is this all right?

TOM JUNIOR.   Fine. Are we through?

RACHEL.   Tomorrow at this time?

TOM JUNIOR.   Fine.

RACHEL.   And the day after?

TOM JUNIOR.   Great. Wait, that's Christmas.

RACHEL.   Would you rather not?

TOM JUNIOR.   No. You work on Christmas?

RACHEL.   I love my work. And try to hold off the sleeping pills for a while, all right?

TOM JUNIOR.   Sure.

RACHEL.   Tomorrow then?

TOM JUNIOR.   Great.

RACHEL.   Tom?... I'm sorry I kept you waiting.

TOM JUNIOR.   Oh, no problem. Oh, I see. Right. Right. Well.... Tomorrow. *(He goes. Rachel moves to the window as "I'll Be Home for Christmas"* plays and snow falls. The lights fade.)*

PROPERTY LIST

Handguns (TOM, MAN)
Wedding ring (RACHEL)
3 drinking glasses (LLOYD)
Package with shower massage
Shoes (POOTY)
Atlas (LLOYD)
Kindling (LLOYD)
Bottle of champagne (TOM, LLOYD)
Large gift box with stuffed animal puppy (TOM)
Glass of milk (LLOYD)
Bag of groceries (RACHEL)
2 bottles of champagne (RACHEL)
TV knob (LLOYD)

SOUND EFFECTS

Crowd response
Doorbell

NEW PLAYS

★ **GUARDIANS by Peter Morris.** In this unflinching look at war, a disgraced American soldier discloses the truth about Abu Ghraib prison, and a clever English journalist reveals how he faked a similar story for the London tabloids. "Compelling, sympathetic and powerful." –*NY Times.* "Sends you into a state of moral turbulence." –*Sunday Times (UK).* "Nothing short of remarkable." –*Village Voice.* [1M, 1W] ISBN: 978-0-8222-2177-7

★ **BLUE DOOR by Tanya Barfield.** Three generations of men (all played by one actor), from slavery through Black Power, challenge Lewis, a tenured professor of mathematics, to embark on a journey combining past and present. "A teasing flare for words." –*Village Voice.* "Unfailingly thought-provoking." –*LA Times.* "The play moves with the speed and logic of a dream." –*Seattle Weekly.* [2M] ISBN: 978-0-8222-2209-5

★ **THE INTELLIGENT DESIGN OF JENNY CHOW by Rolin Jones.** This irreverent "techno-comedy" chronicles one brilliant woman's quest to determine her heritage and face her fears with the help of her astounding creation called Jenny Chow. "Boldly imagined." –*NY Times.* "Fantastical and funny." –*Variety.* "Harvests many laughs and finally a few tears." –*LA Times.* [3M, 3W] ISBN: 978-0-8222-2071-8

★ **SOUVENIR by Stephen Temperley.** Florence Foster Jenkins, a wealthy society eccentric, suffers under the delusion that she is a great coloratura soprano—when in fact the opposite is true. "Hilarious and deeply touching. Incredibly moving and breathtaking." –*NY Daily News.* "A sweet love letter of a play." –*NY Times.* "Wildly funny. Completely charming." –*Star-Ledger.* [1M, 1W] ISBN: 978-0-8222-2157-9

★ **ICE GLEN by Joan Ackermann.** In this touching period comedy, a beautiful poetess dwells in idyllic obscurity on a Berkshire estate with a band of unlikely cohorts. "A beautifully written story of nature and change." –*Talkin' Broadway.* "A lovely play which will leave you with a lot to think about." –*CurtainUp.* "Funny, moving and witty." –*Metroland (Boston).* [4M, 3W] ISBN: 978-0-8222-2175-3

★ **THE LAST DAYS OF JUDAS ISCARIOT by Stephen Adly Guirgis.** Set in a time-bending, darkly comic world between heaven and hell, this play reexamines the plight and fate of the New Testament's most infamous sinner. "An unforced eloquence that finds the poetry in lowdown street talk." –*NY Times.* "A real jaw-dropper." –*Variety.* "An extraordinary play." –*Guardian (UK).* [10M, 5W] ISBN: 978-0-8222-2082-4

DRAMATISTS PLAY SERVICE, INC.
440 Park Avenue South, New York, NY 10016 212-683-8960 Fax 212-213-1539
postmaster@dramatists.com www.dramatists.com

NEW PLAYS

★ **THE GREAT AMERICAN TRAILER PARK MUSICAL music and lyrics by David Nehls, book by Betsy Kelso.** Pippi, a stripper on the run, has just moved into Armadillo Acres, wreaking havoc among the tenants of Florida's most exclusive trailer park. "Adultery, strippers, murderous ex-boyfriends, Costco and the Ice Capades. Undeniable fun." –*NY Post.* "Joyful and un-ashamedly vulgar." –*The New Yorker.* "Sparkles with treasure." –*New York Sun.* [2M, 5W] ISBN: 978-0-8222-2137-1

★ **MATCH by Stephen Belber.** When a young Seattle couple meet a promi-nent New York choreographer, they are led on a fraught journey that will change their lives forever. "Uproariously funny, deeply moving, enthralling theatre." –*NY Daily News.* "Prolific laughs and ear-to-ear smiles." –*NY Magazine.* [2M, 1W] ISBN: 978-0-8222-2020-6

★ **MR. MARMALADE by Noah Haidle.** Four-year-old Lucy's imaginary friend, Mr. Marmalade, doesn't have much time for her—not to mention he has a cocaine addiction and a penchant for pornography. "Alternately hilarious and heartbreaking." –*The New Yorker.* "A mature and accomplished play." –*LA Times.* "Scathingly observant comedy." –*Miami Herald.* [4M, 2W] ISBN: 978-0-8222-2142-5

★ **MOONLIGHT AND MAGNOLIAS by Ron Hutchinson.** Three men cloister themselves as they work tirelessly to reshape a screenplay that's just not working—*Gone with the Wind.* "Consumers of vintage Hollywood insider stories will eat up Hutchinson's diverting conjecture." –*Variety.* "A lot of fun." –*NY Post.* "A Hollywood dream-factory farce." –*Chicago Sun-Times.* [3M, 1W] ISBN: 978-0-8222-2084-8

★ **THE LEARNED LADIES OF PARK AVENUE by David Grimm, trans-lated and freely adapted from Molière's *Les Femmes Savantes.*** Dicky wants to marry Betty, but her mother's plan is for Betty to wed a most pompous man. "A brave, brainy and barmy revision." –*Hartford Courant.* "A rare but welcome bird in contemporary theatre." –*New Haven Register.* "Roll over Cole Porter." –*Boston Globe.* [5M, 5W] ISBN: 978-0-8222-2135-7

★ **REGRETS ONLY by Paul Rudnick.** A sparkling comedy of Manhattan manners that explores the latest topics in marriage, friendships and squandered riches. "One of the funniest quip-meisters on the planet." –*NY Times.* "Precious moments of hilarity. Devastatingly accurate political and social satire." –*BackStage.* "Great fun." –*CurtainUp.* [3M, 3W] ISBN: 978-0-8222-2223-1

DRAMATISTS PLAY SERVICE, INC.
440 Park Avenue South, New York, NY 10016 212-683-8960 Fax 212-213-1539
postmaster@dramatists.com www.dramatists.com

NEW PLAYS

★ **AFTER ASHLEY by Gina Gionfriddo.** A teenager is unwillingly thrust into the national spotlight when a family tragedy becomes talk-show fodder. "A work that virtually any audience would find accessible." *–NY Times.* "Deft characterization and caustic humor." *–NY Sun.* "A smart satirical drama." *–Variety.* [4M, 2W] ISBN: 978-0-8222-2099-2

★ **THE RUBY SUNRISE by Rinne Groff.** Twenty-five years after Ruby struggles to realize her dream of inventing the first television, her daughter faces similar battles of faith as she works to get Ruby's story told on network TV. "Measured and intelligent, optimistic yet clear-eyed." *–NY Magazine.* "Maintains an exciting sense of ingenuity." *–Village Voice.* "Sinuous theatrical flair." *–Broadway.com.* [3M, 4W] ISBN: 978-0-8222-2140-1

★ **MY NAME IS RACHEL CORRIE taken from the writings of Rachel Corrie, edited by Alan Rickman and Katharine Viner.** This solo piece tells the story of Rachel Corrie who was killed in Gaza by an Israeli bulldozer set to demolish a Palestinian home. "Heartbreaking urgency. An invigoratingly detailed portrait of a passionate idealist." *–NY Times.* "Deeply authentically human." *–USA Today.* "A stunning dramatization." *–CurtainUp.* [1W] ISBN: 978-0-8222-2222-4

★ **ALMOST, MAINE by John Cariani.** This charming midwinter night's dream of a play turns romantic clichés on their ear as it chronicles the painfully hilarious amorous adventures (and misadventures) of residents of a remote northern town that doesn't quite exist. "A whimsical approach to the joys and perils of romance." *–NY Times.* "Sweet, poignant and witty." *–NY Daily News.* "Aims for the heart by way of the funny bone." *–Star-Ledger.* [2M, 2W] ISBN: 978-0-8222-2156-2

★ **Mitch Albom's TUESDAYS WITH MORRIE by Jeffrey Hatcher and Mitch Albom, based on the book by Mitch Albom.** The true story of Brandeis University professor Morrie Schwartz and his relationship with his student Mitch Albom. "A touching, life-affirming, deeply emotional drama." *–NY Daily News.* "You'll laugh. You'll cry." *–Variety.* "Moving and powerful." *–NY Post.* [2M] ISBN: 978-0-8222-2188-3

★ **DOG SEES GOD: CONFESSIONS OF A TEENAGE BLOCKHEAD by Bert V. Royal.** An abused pianist and a pyromaniac ex-girlfriend contribute to the teen-angst of America's most hapless kid. "A welcome antidote to the notion that the *Peanuts* gang provides merely American cuteness." *–NY Times.* "Hysterically funny." *–NY Post.* "The *Peanuts* kids have finally come out of their shells." *–Time Out.* [4M, 4W] ISBN: 978-0-8222-2152-4

DRAMATISTS PLAY SERVICE, INC.
440 Park Avenue South, New York, NY 10016 212-683-8960 Fax 212-213-1539
postmaster@dramatists.com www.dramatists.com

NEW PLAYS

★ **RABBIT HOLE by David Lindsay-Abaire.** Winner of the 2007 Pulitzer Prize. Becca and Howie Corbett have everything a couple could want until a life-shattering accident turns their world upside down. "An intensely emotional examination of grief, laced with wit." *—Variety.* "A transcendent and deeply affecting new play." *—Entertainment Weekly.* "Painstakingly beautiful." *—BackStage.* [2M, 3W] ISBN: 978-0-8222-2154-8

★ **DOUBT, A Parable by John Patrick Shanley.** Winner of the 2005 Pulitzer Prize and Tony Award. Sister Aloysius, a Bronx school principal, takes matters into her own hands when she suspects the young Father Flynn of improper relations with one of the male students. "All the elements come invigoratingly together like clockwork." *—Variety.* "Passionate, exquisite, important, engrossing." *—NY Newsday.* [1M, 3W] ISBN: 978-0-8222-2219-4

★ **THE PILLOWMAN by Martin McDonagh.** In an unnamed totalitarian state, an author of horrific children's stories discovers that someone has been making his stories come true. "A blindingly bright black comedy." *—NY Times.* "McDonagh's least forgiving, bravest play." *—Variety.* "Thoroughly startling and genuinely intimidating." *—Chicago Tribune.* [4M, 5 bit parts (2M, 1W, 1 boy, 1 girl)] ISBN: 978-0-8222-2100-5

★ **GREY GARDENS book by Doug Wright, music by Scott Frankel, lyrics by Michael Korie.** The hilarious and heartbreaking story of Big Edie and Little Edie Bouvier Beale, the eccentric aunt and cousin of Jacqueline Kennedy Onassis, once bright names on the social register who became East Hampton's most notorious recluses. "An experience no passionate theatergoer should miss." *—NY Times.* "A unique and unmissable musical." *—Rolling Stone.* [4M, 3W, 2 girls] ISBN: 978-0-8222-2181-4

★ **THE LITTLE DOG LAUGHED by Douglas Carter Beane.** Mitchell Green could make it big as the hot new leading man in Hollywood if Diane, his agent, could just keep him in the closet. "Devastatingly funny." *—NY Times.* "An out-and-out delight." *—NY Daily News.* "Full of wit and wisdom." *—NY Post.* [2M, 2W] ISBN: 978-0-8222-2226-2

★ **SHINING CITY by Conor McPherson.** A guilt-ridden man reaches out to a therapist after seeing the ghost of his recently deceased wife. "Haunting, inspired and glorious." *—NY Times.* "Simply breathtaking and astonishing." *—Time Out.* "A thoughtful, artful, absorbing new drama." *—Star-Ledger.* [3M, 1W] ISBN: 978-0-8222-2187-6

DRAMATISTS PLAY SERVICE, INC.
440 Park Avenue South, New York, NY 10016 212-683-8960 Fax 212-213-1539
postmaster@dramatists.com   www.dramatists.com